A Soldier looks at Spiritual Warfare

A Soldier looks at Spiritual Warfare

Chaplain (Colonel)
Clifford W. Owens

Owens Classic Library

A Soldier Looks at Spiritual Warfare
Copyright © 2017 by Clifford W. Owens

Unless otherwise indicated, Scripture quotations are taken from the King James Version of the Bible

Published by Owens Classic Library

Printed in the United States of America

ISBN: 978-0-692-92262-0

Contents

I dedicate this book to my family. Their spiritual and physical support have enabled me to have this ministry for over 26-years. I thank the LORD for putting us into this ministry. It has been a wonderful tour of duty. All honor belongs to the LORD for His faithfulness. I pray this little book will help you to be victorious in your spiritual battles.

Ephesians 6:10-18

10 Finally, my brethren, be strong in the Lord and in the power of His might.

11 Put on the whole armor of God, that you may be able to stand against the wiles of the devil.

12 For we do not wrestle against flesh and blood, but against principalities, against powers, against the rulers of £the darkness of this age, against spiritual *hosts* of wickedness in the heavenly *places.*

13 Therefore take up the whole armor of God, that you may be able to withstand in the evil day, and having done all, to stand.

14 Stand therefore, having girded your waist with truth, having put on the breastplate of righteousness,

15 and having shod your feet with the preparation of the gospel of peace;

16 above all, taking the shield of faith with which you will be able to quench all the fiery darts of the wicked one.

17 And take the helmet of salvation, and the sword of the Spirit, which is the word of God;

18 praying always with all prayer and supplication in the Spirit, being watchful to this end with all perseverance and supplication for all the saints—

1

Our Operation Order

Some of you have read the book, *A Shepherd Looks at Psalm 23*. As a soldier of 26 years in the chaplaincy, I have often thought it would be helpful to others to write a book and title it, *A Soldier Looks at Spiritual Warfare*. As I began to study and develop first one study, then two studies, then three studies, then 4 studies, and now 5 studies, I realized they are still a work in progress.

I think we have lost the importance of spiritual warfare in our society today because we have growing churches that want to talk about comfort. They want to talk about a life of ease, peace, and joy. But armor is not given out for comfort, it is given out for warfare. Those who have worn body armor know it is not comfortable. It is not comfortable, that is, until shrapnel is flying from artillery or bombs or rifles being fired. Then all of a sudden that armor becomes very comfortable and you would not part with it for anything. So I think I need to lay the basis for our study with the fact that we all need to be warriors.

I read about a senior saint in Joshua 14. His name was Caleb, and he was 85 years old. He said his strength was as good as it was when Moses first called him to serve. Somebody said either he was delusional or he was a wimp. His proclamation was, "Give me this mountain," and at 85 years old, he was ready to lead the charge.

I am convinced there are things for all of us to do in spiritual warfare. We may have an advantage over those who are inexperienced and not battle-tested, but pray that we will all learn together during the next five studies.

Our Father, we are thankful that You have called us to be soldiers of Jesus Christ. We do pray that as we study that You will teach us, help us to report for duty, and to say, "Here am I, Lord. Use me." We live in a time when our churches are not what they once were. Our society certainly is not what it once was. It has been during our watch that there has been great decline. We confess our failure because we have not been the soldiers that we should have been. So direct us and help us to learn all that You have for us. In Jesus' name, amen.

Everything in the military moves because of an operation order. Airplanes do not fly without flight plans. Navy ships do not leave port without a destination. Soldiers do not march unless they have a goal. Likewise, God is giving us an operation order in the above verses. If I still need to sell you on the fact that we are involved in warfare, consider the many other passages in the Scripture dealing with warfare. Paul says in 1 Corinthians 9:26, "Therefore I run thus: not with uncertainty. Thus I fight: not as one who beats the air." He is not like a shadow boxer beating the air, but he has before himself a goal and a purpose and he fights so he can win. Second Corinthians 7:5 reads, "When we were coming to Macedonia our flesh had no rest but we were troubled on every side. Outside were conflicts and inside were fears."

I want to say to you that I don't know if you can ever have fighting without fears. They almost always go together. But "...though we walk in the flesh we do not war according to the flesh. For the weapons of our warfare are not carnal but mighty in God to the pulling down of strongholds" (2 Corinthians 10:3-4a). We have weapons that are adequate to do the job. Paul writes to a young preacher and says, "This charge I commit to you, son Timothy, according to the prophecies previously made concerning you, that by them you may wage the good warfare" (1 Timothy 1:18). Again to Timothy he says, "Fight the good fight of faith. Lay hold on eternal life, to which you were also called and confessed a good confession before many witnesses" (1 Timothy 6:12). And again, "Now therefore endure hardness as a good soldier of Jesus Christ. No man that wars entangles himself with the affairs of this life that he may please him who has chosen him to be a soldier" (2 Timothy 2:3, 4). The faithful soldier, then, can summarize his life, "I have fought the good fight, I have finished my course, I have kept the faith" (2 Timothy 4:7).

Warfare is prominent in the Scriptures. Even in our hymnology we find the importance of Christian warfare. Most of you know *Onward Christian Soldiers* and especially the words:

> Onward, Christian soldiers, marching as to war,
>   With the cross of Jesus going on before.
> Christ, the royal Master, leads against the foe;
>   Forward into battle see His banners go.
>
> Like a mighty army moves the church of God;
> Brothers, we are treading where the saints have trod.
>   We are not divided, all one body we,

A Soldier Looks at Spiritual Warfare

One in hope and doctrine, one in charity.

This is the phrase that challenges me: "Like a mighty army moves the church of God." Do you think it is so today? There was a time when the church held the reins on culture. It is no longer true. The church today is floating along with the culture; culture has integrated our churches and infiltrated them so much that there is not much difference between the church and the culture. Another important hymn on warfare is, *Am I a Soldier of the Cross?*

Am I a soldier of the cross
A follow'r of the Lamb?
And shall I fear to own His cause,
Or blush to speak His name?

Must I be carried to the skies
On flow'ry beds of ease,
While others fought to win the prize,
And sailed through bloody seas?

Are there no foes for me to face?
Must I not stem the flood?
Is this vile world a friend to grace,
To help me on to God?

Sure I must fight if I would reign;
Increase my courage, Lord;
I'll bear the toil, endure the pain,
Supported by Thy Word.

Imagine that you have been promoted to the rank of general. Exciting, right? You are going to go through a "briefing" in each of these five studies.

I have attended many briefings. When the general's staff comes to brief the general officers, they are given the names G1, G2, G3, G4, and G5. This is an easy way to identify the general's staff. It has a particular importance because the G1 is a director of personnel, and that is where this section starts. "Finally brethren" is not talking about the world. Paul is not talking about those who are not in fellowship. He is talking to the brethren.

The G1 comes up to the platform. He introduces himself and gives his greetings to the commanding general. Then he goes through a whole spiel about the troop strength, those who are reporting for duty, and those who are absent. It is during that time that the chaplain, the JAG (judge advocate general), and the medical doctor stand up as special staff and they brief the general. The G1's briefing has to do with the strength of the personnel, including those who are A.W.O.L., those who are in the hospital, and about the morale of the troops. When the G1 is finished he sits down.

Then the G2 comes up to the platform. He is the director of intelligence, and he always starts with the weather report. It is important if we're going to go to war to know whether we can fly or not and what means of travel would be best. Then the next part of his briefing is imperative for success in warfare. He gives the threat of the enemy: What is the enemy's potential; what are his strengths and weaknesses? As the G2, the director of intelligence in the Lord's army says, "We wrestle not against flesh and blood but against principalities, against powers, against spiritual wickedness in high places." The G2 sits down.

The G3 comes up to the platform. He is the director of operations. It is he who sets the plan for battle. He gives the objective for the day. In this passage of Scripture the G3 stands up and says, "Gentlemen, ladies, we have two objectives. Today we are to 'withstand' and we are 'to stand.'" There are only two words in each command and only two objectives. But they are our most important goals.

We must understand what it means to withstand the enemy and also to stand our ground.

The G3 sits down and the G4 comes up. He is the logistics officer. It is he who has control of the beans, bullets, and beds and all the transportation. He gives his report about the supply line. We get our armor from God's supply line. It is supplied to us for combat.

The G4 sits down and the G5 gets up. He is the civil affairs officer. It is he who has the responsibility of changing the hearts of the people. We have all learned that in physical warfare, you can go in and subdue a nation. You can bomb their land until there is nothing left, but not win their hearts. Their hearts have to be changed, or they will forever be the enemy. In spiritual warfare, the word of God and prayer are the only two things that can change people's hearts, and they are all the weapons we need.

In the "briefings" of each of these five studies, you are going to hear from each staff officer. Let's begin with the G1, the "finally brethren."

Now the brethren are a wonderful group of people. I do not know of any I would rather be with than the family of God. But sometimes we find it so comfortable being with this family that we do not even have unsaved friends. In some cases, we never rub shoulders with those outside of our own fellowship. Our fellowships are so comfortable, but there's a whole world of people outside our fellowships who are lost and dying and going to a Christless eternity unless somebody engages them in spiritual warfare. We trust our missionaries to do it. If I were a missionary and asked to give my report after four years of ministry on how many churches have been established, on how many people have been saved, and on how many people have been discipled, it would be fair to ask how many people were saved in our church in the four years I was gone. How many people were baptized in our church during the last four years, and how many people have been discipled? We may be comfortable in our fellowships, but we are not absolved of the responsibility of doing what we can to reach the lost. It is hard to believe that everybody who comes into our church is saved. I wish that it were so, but it's hard to believe. However, they have been given an opportunity to respond to the gospel.

Paul addresses the *brethren*. I think we need to see who these brethren are and then why he would give them such a challenge. They are called saints, and they are called faithful in Christ Jesus. Now that is a mighty important designation. They are also people of grace, and people of peace. They are people who have been blessed beyond all measure. You and I are those brethren. God has blessed us with all spiritual blessings in heavenly places.

If you want to find out how rich you are, you must count up all the blessings you have that money can't buy. I'm glad that these blessings are secure for us in Heaven, where thieves do not break through and steal, moths do not eat holes in the garments, and rust does not corrupt. We have blessings that are secure in heavenly places. We were chosen before the foundation of the world. I was drafted before I was born that I should be holy and without blame. This wonderful group of people have been predestined and they are adopted to be children of God. God predestined us, and He adopted us. Let us never take credit for something that only the grace of God has done. He made me, and He chose me. Although I said "yes" to Him, when I get to heaven, I will not be able to gloat saying, "I did it." He has made me accepted in the Beloved. We all want to be accepted, and in Christ, we are!

We have redemption through His blood and forgiveness of sins. I like the phrase of the song that says, "If you take one step towards the Savior, my friend. You'll find his arms open wide." Thank God that He says, "Come unto me." Can you imagine that the Creator and Sustainer of the universe says, "Come" and He receives all who come?

He has made known unto us the mystery of His will. What was concealed in the Old Testament is now revealed in the New Testament. We know so much more than what Abraham and Moses and all the prophets knew because of the completed Word of God. He has made known unto us His purposes. We have obtained an inheritance. I don't know anyone who would miss the reading of a will if that person were on the receiving end of the will. He would have to be sick in the hospital or something similar to not be there to find out what is his inheritance.

I want to tell you that God has already told us that our heritage is eternal life with Jesus and with the family of God forever and ever. Wow! What an inheritance. We were sealed with that Holy Spirit of promise. We know that we are saved because the Spirit Himself bears witness with our spirit that we are the sons of God. How thrilling it is to be part of the brethren and to know for sure that we've been sealed. We've been authenticated. It is the real thing.

The mark of the people of faith is their love for all of the saints. That was the grand mark of the Christians in the early church. They were known for how they loved one another. The brethren cared for one another. They were aware of His great power toward them who believe. He has quickened us who were dead in trespasses—He has made us alive. Dead soldiers are not of any value. You have to be able to stand on your feet, be to able to function, and be able to carry on the work. He has raised us up together and made us sit in heavenly places in Christ Jesus. Some of you have sung the song, *Heaven came down and Glory filled my soul*. I suppose that might be a little taste of what this is. I know that on Saturday nights when I had the responsibility of preaching two times the next Sunday, I would put on some good gospel songs, and I would sit, listen, pray, and meditate. It was marvelous how God would minister, strengthen, and prepare me for the ministry of the coming day. God has done that for many saints in His household. We are all part of the army. We are built upon the foundation of the apostles and prophets, Jesus Christ Himself being the chief Cornerstone, and so we have a great foundation.

Soldiers will tell you that the most important time of their training was the time they disliked the most: basic training. The story is told about the sergeant who was giving a recruit a very hard time. He said to him at his graduation, "When I die, you likely will come and spit on my grave." The troop spoke up and said, "No, sergeant. That's not true. I made up my mind that when I get out of this army, I'll never stand in line again." But when that soldier faces combat, the foundation laid by that drill instructor will be of great value in his life.

The Ephesians failed the most important test of all. They left their first love. In 1 Corinthians 10:12, Paul says, "Wherefore let him who thinks that he stands, take heed lest he falls." We think we are so strong that we can survive any combat or any fiery darts of the enemy. However, every one of us has the potential of falling. Paul says, "I command you to be strong in the Lord."

I have meditated on this many times. How can it be that with all the qualities of the Ephesians mentioned in chapter one, Paul would say, "Strengthen yourselves?" We all need to make sure that we are sharpening our skills, and we need to make sure that we are using them. After listing those wonderful qualities in the first part of the book, then he says to this group of people who have not yet fallen out of love, "Be strong." Going from the positional, from where I know I am in Christ, to the practical is difficult. How to get my feet to do what my mind and heart know is right is sometimes a challenge.

Let me give you some areas in which we need to strengthen ourselves. Strengthening in these areas will help us in the transition from the positional to the practical. First of all we need to yield ourselves to God and not serve the world, the flesh, or the devil (1 John 2:15-17). We need to know that these are our natural enemies. I need constantly to be yielding myself to God.

In the military, when active-duty guys get like me, old, grey-haired, and wearing glasses, we called them "ROADS." R.O.A.D. stands for Retired On Active Duty— someone who is no longer contributing, but just biding his time until retirement. Have you ever known anybody retired on active duty? I know pastors like that, and missionaries like that, and deacons like that. And I have wanted to be like that. So I need strengthening to make sure that I yield myself to God and that I take my stand day by day against those three enemies. I need to challenge them in Jesus' name. I need to deny myself and look out for the good of others. Jesus said in Matthew 16:24, "If any man will come after me, let him deny himself, and take up his cross, and follow me." In this world of affluence and comfort, it is so easy *not* to deny ourselves. We need to be looking out for the good of others. Where there is a fallen brother and where there is a person living in sin, we need to help. We need constant help to accept the lordship of Christ in every area of our lives and activities.

The world has changed a lot in my 60 years of ministry. People have not understood the whole principle of lordship. He has a right to call every step. The steps of a righteous man are ordered of the Lord, so whether it is a business decision, a social function, a church activity, or a family situation, we need His direction. You and I need to make sure that this is our number one priority.

Lastly, we must obey Him. It is pretty easy to say, "Wait Lord, just wait," when all the time He is saying, "Now!" Our provision is the whole armor of God. We will look more at that as we proceed. But for now, understand and appreciate what our position is in Christ. It is wonderful, and we don't want to ever shrink back from Him. Let us understand that this is not a playground but a battleground in which we live. I suspect that the battle is going to become fierce in the near future, so we need to be ready and be good soldiers of Jesus Christ.

Let's pray together.

Father, how thankful I am that You called us, You saved us, and You redeemed us. You called us to be witnesses for You. It is so easy in the flesh to retire on active duty. I pray that You will help us to see areas where we can help in the battle, whether it is going to battle ourselves or as support for others who do pull the trigger. Help us to see the importance of the battle before us and make sure that we are strong in the Lord. For it's in His Name I pray, amen.

2

Our Intelligence Report

The G2 is the director of intelligence. When he comes to the podium he gives the intelligence report. That is where we are in this study. He always starts out with the weather because it is very important to operations. Then he turns to a very serious matter. He identifies the enemy and his threat to our operation. Similarly, Paul does that for us. Verse 12 warns us, "For we do not wrestle against flesh and blood, but against principalities, against powers, against the rulers of the darkness of this age, against spiritual hosts of wickedness in the heavenly places." We have a formidable foe that we must face.

Our Father, we realize this is a very, very important section for us. In the day and age in which we are living, we are bombarded by the forces of evil. You have dropped us into this situation, maybe behind enemy lines. You ask us to be strong in the Lord, to put on the battle uniform, to take the offensive, and to accomplish

Your will. So would You help us as we think about this passage? Help us to be able to make application to our personal walk so that we, indeed, will be alert to the enemy around us. Help us to take our position on the line of battle and to serve You. In Jesus' name, amen.

Every battle has what is called a T.O.C. It stands for a "Tactical Operations Center." Inside that building or tent is a situation board, and that situation board outlines everything that the G2 wants to say to the general. I'll never forget one particular day when my observation in the T.O.C. of what was on the situation board probably saved my life. My responsibility was to cover a large area of operations, and my main base in that area was Pleiku, Vietnam. The next place was Kontum, which was about 20 miles away. In big bold letters, with scallops all the way around it, read, "Imminent Danger of an Ambush." Well that's exciting when you're going to go 20 miles down a long road through the mountains to a place called Kontum. I had a brand new assistant, so I came back to my assistant and said, "If we get hit today, I want to know what you are going to do."

"Well, Chaplain," he said, "if we get hit, I'm going to slam on the brakes, and we're going to jump out of our quarter ton jeep. We're going to get in the ditch, and we're going to return fire."

I put my finger on his nose, and I said, "Son, let me tell you something. If you take your foot off the accelerator, I'll break your leg."

You see, the important thing in an ambush is to get out of the kill zone. You don't want to hang around inside the kill zone. So that day we were lined up by the MP's. They always lined us up, and they saw the cross on the Jeep. They said, "Chaplain, you ride right behind us." Everybody wanted a chaplain to ride nearby. They thought that would be a good luck charm. They had a big, heavy armored vehicle, and they put our little quarter-ton jeep behind it. The next vehicle behind us was a big petroleum tanker. Then a whole bunch of other vehicles followed behind in a convoy. There was a major explosion off to my right. It took me by surprise because it was in an open field. Then all of a sudden the air just broke loose with machine gun fire, mortar fire, and Rocket-propelled Grenades. In fact, an RPG round got the tanker behind us and blew it up in the middle of the road. That stranded several people in the middle of the kill zone, and we took casualties. It was a bad day!

I have often wondered what would have happened if I had not been alert to the situation or if my brand new driver would have stopped as he told me he would do. We know he should have had better training, but that is why the situation board was so important. Our situation board, God's word, tells us what you and I are going to face this week. What happened that day on the road to Kontum is a small thing compared to what you and I will face in our daily warfare.

Some of you who are older remember the warfare we used to have. It was called F.E.B.A. or "forward edge of the battle area." Many of you have seen Revolutionary War and Civil War battle films and have seen the lineup of the troops as they marched toward one another. They were the forward edge of the battle. It is not like that today. We live in a day of guerrilla warfare. If the enemy does not have an advantage, he does not want to fight. He does not want to identify himself. I will never forget the first time I saw an individual in black pajamas with a straw hat carrying an AK-47. He was probably our friend in the daytime, but at night he might have been shooting at us. That is the way it is today, but we have an enemy who is very clearly defined for us in the Scripture. I don't want to give him credit he does not deserve because he is not God. We need to recognize our dependence upon being strong in the Lord and putting on the armor of God.

Second Corinthians 2:11 is a very important verse. "Lest he should get an advantage of us; we are not ignorant of his devices." Is it not interesting that in every generation people come along the trail and bump their toes on the same old rock. Certainly, things get renamed and redefined, but there is really "nothing new under the sun." It is old philosophy readdressed. It is old lies repackaged. Satan has a number of tricks that he uses on humans. Devil means "accuser." In Revelation 12:7-11, he is called the "accuser of the brethren." Now, sometimes he tells the truth about us. He says, "God, did You see what Your child did?" God is able to say, "Yes, I saw that. I want you to know it's under the blood. It's been confessed and forgiven, and it's all behind him." I want to say that sometimes the devil lies about it when he accuses us before God. He did that when he accused Job. He was lying. He did not know the truth about Job. Our enemy whose name is the devil is the accuser. Satan means "adversary," and he is the enemy of God and His people. The devil always makes wonderful promises. He wants to appear as our friend, but I want to say to you that he is never our friend. He never has your best interest nor the glory of God in view. He only has himself and evil as his goal, and so he is our adversary.

It is interesting how he is described in Scripture. He is described in Matthew 4:3 as the tempter. Have you ever wondered where some thoughts come from? You might even be having devotions, and all of a sudden a horrible thought comes flooding through your mind. It is not pleasing to you, and you know it is not pleasing to God. Where did it come from? Always remember that our adversary takes every advantage of us.

The tempter came to Jesus and said, "If You are the Son of God, command that these stones become bread." Every time I read that phrase, knowing that Jesus Christ is the Son of God, I am disturbed because Satan wants to cast doubt. "If You are really the Son of God, command these stones to be bread." If you have been hungry a long time, would that not seem like a rather innocent request? Jesus understood it was not innocent because Satan is the adversary, and he wanted to cause sin.

He is also described in the Scripture as a murderer and a liar. In John 8:44, Jesus said to the Pharisees, "You are of your father the devil, and the desires of your father you want to do. He was a murderer from the beginning, and does not stand in the truth because there is no truth in him. When he speaks a lie, he speaks from his own resources for he is a liar and the father of it." I don't know if you are as appalled as I am at our news broadcasts and our papers that come to our homes week after week. They bring accounts of murder after murder and lies upon lies. Where did that all come from? It did not come from God nor from God's children. Satan is behind the whole program. He is having a heyday today.

He is called a lion in 1 Peter 5:8. "Be sober, be vigilant; because your adversary the devil walks about as a roaring lion, seeking whom he may devour." Now if he always roared and gave us the alert, it would be easier to identify him than in some of the forms he takes. He was called the serpent in Genesis 3:1, and after that he was called the angel of light. The lion roars for destruction. When we recall the account in Genesis 3:1 about the serpent's encounter with Adam and Eve, we see he was more subtle than any of the beasts of the field. He comes again and casts just a little doubt. "Has God indeed said...?" He wants to twist the truth and make it into a lie. The devil is very clever. He is more clever than I am and more clever than you are. I think he could wear a clerical collar. He may look like an angel of light. According to Second Corinthians 11:13-15; "False apostles and deceitful workers transform themselves into apostles of Christ. This is no wonder! For Satan himself transforms himself into an angel of light. Therefore it is no great thing if his ministers also transform themselves into ministers of righteousness, whose end will be according to their works."

It has been a delight for me during some of the years of ministry to see other preachers come to the Lord. An exciting time I will never forget is when I was first transferred to Florida. We went to Punta Gorda, and I was stationed at Tampa. There was a head chaplain, but I outranked him. I was there in an advisory role. He was the brigade chaplain and was a wonderful guy. He was especially kind, courteous, and thoughtful. Soon after I got there his daughter was killed in a car wreck. He came to me and said, "Chaplain Cliff, you know what, I have no hope." What a tragedy for this wonderful human being, who appeared as an angel, but said, "There is no hope in me." I was able to introduce him to Christ. That was a thrill, but I want you to know that in America, on our television screens, in our media, and in every other place, there are those who are representing the enemy, not God.

We need to remember that Satan performs as an angel of light. He is called the god of this world, and he has blinded the eyes of them who believe not. Every time there is a gospel presentation, he likes to be there. He can only be one place at a time, but legions of demons work for him. He is well organized and is able to cause distraction. He is the one who makes the mind wander all over the place. That is not too difficult since most speakers speak at around 300 words a minute and our minds clip along at 600 words a minute. We need to know his goal. He is our enemy and our adversary. He appears in different forms.

He is full of trickery. His goal today is to oppose all that is of God and to exalt himself above God.

He likes to make warfare, and he is very good at war. He has had many years of experience. We come on the scene as one generation, but he has been around for many generations. Paul really targets our warfare. He says, "Though we walk in the flesh, we do not war according to the flesh. For the weapons of our warfare are not carnal but mighty in God for pulling down strongholds, casting down arguments and every high thing that exalts itself against the knowledge of God, bringing into captivity every wandering thought to the obedience of Christ." Second Corinthians 10:3-5 reminds us that Satan is here to steal away the truth. He is here to make us falter and be ineffective in our role of combat.

He wants to exalt himself. We need to look at that a moment. In John 12:31 Jesus said, "Now is the judgment of this world; now shall the prince of this world be cast out." Then He said in John 14:30, "I will no longer talk much with you for the prince of this world is coming, and he has nothing in me." Then in John 16, Jesus said that the Holy Spirit would come and convict the world of...judgment because the prince of this world is judged. Satan knows he is judged. The prince of this world is already under sentence. One day God is going to take care of him forever and ever, and not only him, but also all of his followers.

Let us look at some people who met him face-to-face. The person who had the first encounter with him was Eve. Satan changed his appearance and came to her as a serpent with subtlety, lying, and deception. He said to the woman, "Has God said?" As a result of that question Eve began to question the goodness of God. She began to question God's authority. She began to question whether God really had her best interest at heart, so she took of the fruit. I often say to people, "The problem was not in the apple on the tree but with the pair on the ground." Those two, both Adam and Eve, were deceived and sinned. She began to question God. In Matthew 16:23, the Lord spoke to Peter, "Get behind Me, Satan! You are an offense to Me, for you are not mindful of the things of God, but the things of men." In Luke 22:31, the Lord also said, "Simon, Simon! behold, Satan has desired to have you, that he may sift you as wheat." Since the devil wanted to attack a servant of God, Peter was a great one to attack.

The story about Ananias and Sapphira in Acts chapter 5 is one that you all know well. When Ananias lied about the sale of the property, Peter said to him, "Why has Satan filled your heart to lie to the Holy Spirit and keep back part of the price of land for yourself?" He attributes the lying to Satan himself. Paul says in 1 Thessalonians 2:18, "We wanted to come to you—even I, Paul, time and again—but Satan hindered us." Now whether it was only Satan who did that or his band of demons who did it, I don't know. But I do know that Satan was behind it. Have you ever been hindered? Second Corinthians 2:11 tells us we are not ignorant of his methods. He is full of trickery. He has all sorts of ways in which he likes to attack us. I listed some that I have encountered in my years of combat. He lies, he deceives, he counterfeits, he accuses, and he hinders. I suppose he is still working in the new age movement and humanism, and he is still finding ways to oppose God and his children. He is full of trickery.

Let me give you the gist of a letter a missionary sent to one of his supporting churches. He wrote, "Dear brethren, thank you for praying bombs!" He wrote about the work project that they were involved in. He went through a whole list of things they tried to do, and in every detail, he said "but Satan hindered us." Then he said, "Thanks for praying bombs. People took sick and we were short in personnel and Satan hindered. Thanks for praying bombs."

He went through four things in that letter that happened, and lastly he said, "We just want you to know that at the end of that week of service many people came to Christ."

I want you to know that we have a persistent enemy. After the temptation of Jesus, Satan departed from Him for a season. I think the next time we really see his attack is in Gethsemane. I am sure there were other attacks, but I think it was a big attack at Gethsemane. Satan waged war against the Lord Jesus. We have a persistent enemy, but I want you to understand that he is doomed. He may win an occasional skirmish, but he is not going to win the battle. We all know of times when he won a skirmish. We had to fall on our knees and cry out to God for mercy. We had to ask for forgiveness and pray on the armor of God once again in order to move forward.

James 4:7 is a verse that I will remember until the Lord calls me home. Some of you may remember Dr. Gerard Knol. He was the pastor at Lake Drive Baptist Church in Grand Rapids, Michigan. He was a little Dutchman who had ears that seemed to be indicators of his blood pressure. Ordinations had not been going well in Grand Rapids. Space does not permit going into all of things that were said at my ordination, but it finally came to this question from Dr. Knol: "Mr. Owens, do you have victory over the devil?" If I had said "yes," it would have sounded like I was full of pride. I hesitated. "Well," he said, "Do you have any support verses for victory over the devil?" Standing on my feet in my ordination service was challenging, but my mind quickly searched for a Bible verse. I said, "Resist the devil and he will flee from you." I could see his ears getting red. After a while (I felt it was a two-minute pause) he said, "Is there anything else?" My mind started going again and the computer started running. "Submit yourselves to God," I said, "Resist the devil and he will flee from you." He said, "Don't you ever forget it."

29

I want to say to you, for this day's battle and for the days that are ahead, God wants us to win the victory. He has made every provision possible for us. We must put on the armor. When I put on the armor, I am submitting to God. I am ready for combat. I will resist the devil, and he will flee from me. James says, "Draw near to God and He will draw near to you." That is my prayer for myself and for each one reading this. Let us pray together.

Father, how important it is to understand that our enemy is on a leash. He is not to be victorious, but we are to be victorious by Your grace. So I pray that we will not lead lives of defeat but lives of victory. The battle is not ours, but it is Yours. We submit to You and ask of You grace sufficient for this day and for this week of combat. In Jesus' name, amen.

3

Our Objective

The G3 now briefs us on our objective in Ephesians 6:13-14. "Wherefore, take unto you the whole armor of God, that you may be able to withstand in the evil day, and having done all, to stand. Stand, therefore, having your loins girded about with truth, and having on the breastplate of righteousness." We have two areas of responsibility, and they are to withstand and then to stand. We always have to have an objective. Some of you have observed warfare in your living room on TV. The newscaster said, "Today the troops were taking Hill 678."

You probably wondered, "What in the world is Hill 678?" That number is the elevation. The objectives are given by elevation or by some key terrain feature.

Objectives are given to see God's direction and to be able to accomplish His will for the future. Objectives to withstand and to stand in this passage of Scripture are emphasized. I want to teach you two Greek words. *Anthistemi* is the word for "withstand." It means to "stand against." The other is *histemi*, which means to "stand." The first objective is to **withstand** or resist. It is the same word that is translated in James 4:7. "Submit yourselves therefore to God, resist (*anthistami*) the devil and he will flee from you." This area of resisting is not pleasant. We do not like confrontation. It is often difficult to call people on the carpet or to "tell it the way it is" because we want to be liked by everybody. God has put us in the midst of the fight to be able to resist, and I have to say, that is frightening. When I think about it, I remember my early years as a seminary student. We had a Bible Conference in Grand Rapids, Michigan. Dr. Robert Ketchum came and told us about the early years in the formation of our General Association of Regular Baptist Churches. I mean, there was a fight! There was resistance. It was going on in our churches. When is the last time you heard anything about standing up for righteousness?

My Facebook friends are telling me about the movies they are going to see and how wonderful they are. It is the same group of friends who went to see Mel Gibson's *The Passion Of The Christ*. After the movie, he gave thousands of dollars to the Roman Catholic Church, and his personal life completely fell apart. People were praising Hollywood. We do not hear the philosophy of Hollywood being condemned today. God says to me, "Clifford, I have placed you behind enemy lines today, and I don't want you to sit down and just go on vacation the rest of your life. I want you to resist." I tried to think of principles I learned in my military experience that have taught me how to resist. How can I best do that? I think there are insights I can share with you.

First of all, you have to know where you are. Paul says in 2 Corinthians 11:23a, "For I received from the Lord that which I also delivered to you." He had a standing before the Lord. He knew exactly who it was he was serving and he knew exactly where he was in the fight. We have to know where we are. A few years back we were in an army training exercise. I was going down the road with my driver in the quarter ton jeep, and as I looked ahead of us, I saw a soldier in full battle gear. He was a second lieutenant, and he was crying. I said to my assistant, "Stop. We'll see what's going on."

We stopped and I said, "What's wrong?"

He said, "We had an objective that we were supposed to meet on hill 235. We were supposed to take the hill. My platoon was held in reserve and another platoon was to be the attacking platoon. Another order came down from headquarters, and they changed our order at the last moment. I wasn't with my platoon, and they were ordered to be the attacking platoon. They went off and left me, and I don't know where they are!"

I looked at him smiling and said, "I know where they are. Would you like me to take you to them?"

I took him up so he could join his platoon and take leadership again.

That night we had a special function, and all the officers were there. I went to the general, who was a Christian, and I told him he had a second lieutenant who needed a little TLC. He looked at me and smiled and asked what happened. I told him what had happened. He laughed and said, "You know, when I was a second lieutenant, I lost my platoon."

We have to know where we are in this fight. The Infantry motto is "Follow me." You will have a difficult time resisting if you do not know where you stand.

I do not want to take a lot of time on this since we spent the whole study on it last time, but we have to know who our enemy is lest he should get an advantage over us. We are not ignorant of his devices. I am just amazed at how people in every generation have to bump their toes on the same old hard rock on the same old path. Why can we not learn so we will be able to understand the enemy? He is putting up a fight today. Watch the broadcasts, and read the news. You also can observe Satan's influence as you walk in any mall.

There is so much of his influence going on in this world today and, sadly, it is going on in our churches. I have been in contact with our state representative in Michigan, talking to him about the possibility of an interim ministry for the summer. He said, "Cliff, there is just so much unrest and so much trouble in our churches."

Why? It is because the enemy is putting up a fight. He does not want us to succeed.

I spoke with a fellow pastor at a missions meeting recently, and asked him about a couple that we love who were in his church.

He said, "They left when a whole bunch of people left with our former pastor. The church split."

That happens over and over again. I am afraid the song being sung, rather than *You Bring the One Next to You and I'll Bring the One Next to Me*, is "You split the one next to you, and I'll split the one next to me. In no time at all we'll split them all." We have to know about the devices of the enemy.

The enemy is not one another. It is no help if we are killed by friendly fire. I remember a night out in the jungle when all of a sudden the artillery was coming in way too close. The company commander was yelling on the radio trying to get the artillery stopped. We knew it had to be our own artillery, and they needed to get it shut down before it wiped us out. We later came to find out that they did not know we were in that quadrant. Some of you may know Chaplain Stan Beach. He has a cochlear implant and he has an artificial leg. He was hit in that very same area by friendly fire. I want you to know where you are and where you are firing your shots.

We must not fire at one another. Sometimes we kill brothers because we do not understand who it is that we are fighting. We have to know why we are soldiers of Jesus Christ. We join the Lord's army to please Him who has chosen us to be soldiers. It is always a fearful thing to see a family member go to war. It was easier for me to go than to see my son and my grandson go. I engraved a plaque for my son who is now a general. I said to him when I gave it to him, "I want you to understand this verse engraved on the plaque, "No man that wars entangles himself in the affairs of this life, that he may please Him who has chosen him to be a soldier'" (2 Timothy 2:4). I said, "I want you to remember who it is that you are serving."

Why are we soldiers? We are soldiers because He called us. We have to answer His call and give ourselves to be His soldiers if we are going to fight a good fight. If we are going to do this, we must remember our objective.

Paul stated at the end of his life, "I have finished my course, I have kept the faith." That is what we want to do. The most important words we could hear are, "Well done thou good and faithful servant." Paul looked forward to that. He looked forward to being able to give that accountability. "I have finished my course, I have kept the faith." I've been a good soldier of Jesus Christ.

We will never resist unless we keep a proper perspective. God has for me a crown of righteousness which the Lord, the righteous judge will give me on that day—not to me only but to all them that love His appearing. I pray for the day when the Church of Jesus Christ will march like a mighty army. We have lost so many skirmishes. Can you remember earlier days when Wednesday night was reserved for church functions? Now it is an athletic night. Every possible activity to distract from the ministry of the church takes place in the public schools on Wednesday nights. We have taken the Bible out of the school and we have taken prayer out of the school. Our schools are quick to give different things for the kids to be involved in, and our churches have watched it happen.

I would like to recommend a DVD to you. Its title is, *The Last Ounce of Courage*. Members of a whole community, except one, just quietly stand silent and watch their liberties taken from them. The one exception is the mayor of the city, who is a Christian. He finally sees the handwriting on the wall and takes on the ACLU. It is a tearjerker, but it is worth watching.

Not only are we to resist, but we are to **stand** (*histemi*). Our policy in Iraq is an example of resisting but not standing. For example, we have gone into some areas, and we have resisted. We took towns and then pulled out. The enemy came right back into those towns. It is not enough to resist only. We have to hold what we have taken. During my first six months in Vietnam, that was how we operated. Every two weeks we went into the DMZ and cleaned it out. We took casualties and caused a lot of casualties on the other side. Then we would pull back and have memorial services, take care of the equipment, and get ready for another mission. Two weeks later we would go back in and do the same dumb thing again. It was the politicians who had control. It was not the generals but the politicians who sent us to fight and then to do the worst thing which was to pull back. The army has a very neat way of talking about retreat, although in principle the army knows nothing about retreat. The word is not in the army's vocabulary. However, the army has what they call a strategic withdrawal.

We are retreating all over the place. Would to God that we would learn how to have a strategic withdrawal. Would to God that we would learn not only to resist but then to occupy or "stand." We have this word in some of the verses I have outlined. To stand before the Son of Man is to continue to stand. In Romans 5:2, Paul says, "Through whom also we have access by faith into this grace in which we stand, and rejoice in hope of the glory of God." This is a firm footing. From 1 Corinthians 15:1-2, "Moreover, brethren, I declare to you the gospel which I preached to you, which also you received and in which you stand, by which also you are saved, if you hold fast that word which I preached to you—unless you believed in vain." And in 2 Corinthians 1:20, "For by faith you stand." Again, it is stability that is necessary. Peter says it is the grace of God "Wherein we stand." Let me give you some help. I think it is important to learn how to stand. First of all, we have to understand we are not alone. Sometimes we feel rather isolated. It is quite easy to stand when we are in a group of like-minded people. But put alone on some street corner, and it is a different story.

Elijah had that problem after his great experience on Mount Carmel where he saw fire coming down out of heaven, licking up all the water in the trenches, burning the sacrifice and even the stones. Then he told Ahab he had better get going because it was going to rain. Then he did the 22-mile run down the hill. He was at the entrance of Jezreel when Ahab told Jezebel all he had done and how he had killed all of the prophets. She sent word to him that she would have his life the next day. Now Elijah just wanted to die. He could have stayed one more day and Jezebel would have taken care of that, but he ran for his life.

After time in a cave, he went out and said to the Lord, "I have been very zealous for the Lord God of hosts; because the children of Israel have forsaken Your covenant, torn down Your altars, and killed Your prophets with the sword. I alone am left; and they seek to take my life" (2 Kings 19:14). So there was a little meeting with God, and God said to Elijah, "Yet I have reserved seven thousand in

Israel, all whose knees have not bowed to Baal, and every mouth that has not kissed him" (2 Kings17:18). There were 7,000 men who had never doubted the Lord. You would think that one of those men could have run across the path of Elijah and could have been an encouragement and a help to him.

I have been in some of those isolated places where I really did not feel the fellowship of the brethren or the support of a brother. Some missionaries know what that is like. I praise the Lord for every missionary that can go into a place where there is no established church and begin a brand new church. I am afraid that I do not have it in me to do that. My hat goes off to those who do it all alone. The missionary starts first with a Bible study with one or two families. Then he sees that little group begin to grow. If you think you are going to be alone today you will not stand very long. Elijah felt he wanted to die because he felt he was all alone. I want to remind you that one with God is a majority.

David is a good example of that. I would like to have heard him say when he went out to meet his brothers, "Who is this uncircumcised Philistine?" David was going to take a stand even though alone, but God was with him. I want to encourage you. God may put each of us in a place where we may not have a lot of support around us. He is always there, and He says to us, "I want you to stay and be faithful during your watch."

One of my most important times in Vietnam was when I went out at night and visited the men keeping watch at different posts. We were in a defensive posture, and we had a perimeter set up. I liked to go to those places where they were on watch and say to those young men,

"How's it going?"

"Well, okay Chaplain."

"Do you have any prayer requests tonight?"

"Well, yeah."

So then they would open up their hearts. It was a great opportunity to talk to those young guys. After I finished ministering to them I would say this,

"I want you to stay awake tonight."

Why did I want them to stay awake? I know what happens when the enemy penetrates the perimeter and gets inside. I have observed that too.

We have to be faithful during our watch. I do not have to do somebody else's watch. I just have to worry about my responsibility and my assignment. I must make sure that when I am given that commission I am there. I must stay there until God relieves me. What would happen if a guard at the main gate would say, "Well, my time is up," and leave his post?

I like the story of the young recruit that was fresh out of basic training. The command did not know where to put him, so they put him out on the backside of the army post.

They said, "No one who comes along this road is to be let through this gate unless he can say the password." He was about to fall asleep because nothing was happening. They put him out there because nobody came that way, but he looked up to see this sedan coming. On the front of this sedan was a red license plate with 4 gold stars on it. The young recruit stood at attention. He knew it was a general, and he gave the challenger word. The general did not reply and so the young soldier said the challenge word again. The general said,

"Son, I don't know the password."

The young man said, "General you can't go in."

The General replied "I'm going to go in."

"Well sir," the young man said, "before you go in, I've got a question. When you start driving, I want to know, do I shoot you first or your driver?"

He was going to stay there and do his job, no matter what.

And we are to stay where God has placed us until He relieves us. Some of us may be getting weak-kneed, but we are still in the ministry of occupying. Some of you have a greater prayer ministry. It is greater now than it has ever been in your life. I want you to understand how important you are as you stand for Jesus Christ.

We are to keep a proper perspective. Matthew 25:21 says, "His lord said to him, 'Well done, good and faithful servant; you were faithful over a few things, I will make you ruler over many things. Enter into the joy of your lord.'" The celebration is coming soon.

As I conclude, I want to say that I really believe this statement: "If a person doesn't stand for something he will fall for anything." It is so important in the day and age in which we live to learn how to resist by God's grace. I am talking about a resistance that understands the enemy's tactics and what he is doing and then stands in opposition to the enemy. It is very important that we have a proper standing before this generation and before the Lord.

I have thought about this a lot recently. Do our children hold the same values that we hold? Does the church have the same values and ministry today that it did when you started in it however many years ago? Things are in tremendous change. We have a choice. We can choose to stand up and fight for righteousness, or we can be swept away.

Our objective today is to withstand and to stand.

Father, we are so thankful that you have called us to be a good soldier of Jesus Christ. It is our heart's desire, Father, that we would fulfill all righteousness in obeying your word. I am listening to our commander, the Lord Jesus. This day some may be trapped "behind enemy lines" and may feel all alone. Yet we realize we are never alone when we are with you. So help us to do our part in resisting and standing. In Jesus' name, amen.

4

Our Defensive Armor

A lot of people are impressed with the title, Colonel, but I want you to know that to the chaplain his title, Chaplain, is far more important than his rank. A corporal has more command and authority than a chaplain colonel because the chaplain does not have command authority. However, he is a very powerful man in the military because he can go wherever he wants, when necessary, without going through the chain of command. If he is wise, he will work through the chain of command, but chaplain is a very powerful title. A captain chaplain serves a battalion, a major chaplain serves a brigade, and a full colonel serves a division.

You may have heard or even taught lessons on Ephesians 6:14-18, but I'd like to give you some insights on this passage from a military perspective.

Let us pray.

Father, how grateful we are to be part of the family of God, and we are grateful that You have enlisted us to be soldiers for Jesus Christ. We thank You that You have provided everything that is needed for us to be good soldiers. We have our defensive armor, and we have our offensive weapons. So I am praying that as we study the Word once again the Holy Spirit who wrote this might also instruct us and teach us and help us to make application in our personal walk. May we be victorious in the battle in which You have called us to participate. In Jesus' name, amen.

It is vitally important that we understand our defensive armor. The G4 is the one that has control of all the equipment. When the soldier goes to the supply room, he is issued a helmet and the web gear with all of the attachments that go on it. He is issued body armor called the flak jacket. He is issued a gas mask which would be equivalent to the shield in New Testament times. Then lastly he is given a weapon by serial number. He is responsible at all times for that weapon.

After he gets all his equipment from the supply office he is ready to assemble it, practice with it, and use it when he goes into war. The Scripture talks about our defensive armor in Ephesians 6:14-18. "Stand therefore, having girded your waist with truth, having put on the breastplate of righteousness, and having shod your feet with the preparation of the gospel of peace; above all, taking the shield of faith with which you will be able to quench all the fiery darts of the wicked one. And take the helmet of salvation, and the sword of the Spirit, which is the word of God."

The very best offense is a good defense. Many of you are basketball fans. The commentator talks a lot about the defense because you can score 100 points, but if you do not stop the other team from scoring 102, you are going to lose the game.

Likewise, it is important that we have a strong defense. God has given us five defensive and two offensive parts of the armor. We need to treasure these, and since we're fighting an enemy of the spirit world, we need special equipment. Here is something I want you to ponder: God gives us armor, not for comfort, but for combat. Those who have put on all this armor know it is not comfortable. When we have training, we put all of it on. We know we are not going to be fighting, so it is easy to ask the question, "Why do we have to wear this helmet?" That helmet weighs almost eight pounds, and you know it does things to your hair. When it is hot, that body armor makes it feel a lot hotter. It does not breathe, and it is terribly uncomfortable underneath that body armor. So the soldier is always trying to figure out ways that he can cheat. Sometimes he would take the steel pot off (today it's not steel, but a composite) and would cover the liner with a camouflage cover and put it on. That weighs about one pound, and it feels so much better. But I want to tell you that when the fire is real, you cannot get enough of that armor on. You never have to remind a soldier going into a firefight to put on his armor.

One of my great concerns today is that the churches have begun to seek only a friendly posture. We are telling people about all the benefits of the gospel, which are wonderful, but we are not called merely to enjoy benefits of the gospel. We are called to be a part of the army of God and to stand up and fight against the forces of wickedness. We need to tell new converts that the battle starts today because it really does. The devil does not give in easily. He immediately begins to go after that new believer.

I want to say something about ammo pouches, which are used to carry ammunition for a soldier's weapon. The chaplain does not carry a M16. He has an assistant who is supposed to be his bodyguard. My ammo pouches were filled with Gideon New Testaments. I handed out cases of them during the year I spent in Vietnam. There was a lot of humidity, a lot of filth, and a lot of dirt, so they needed to be replaced after a while when they were not usable, so I just kept passing them out. The Catholic chaplain happened to notice the guys coming to me and getting all those New Testaments. He said to me, "Hey Cliff, could I pass out those New Testaments?"

I said, "Well, I have a case I will give you." I gave him a case of them, and he started handing out New Testaments.

Let us consider the girdle of truth. Nothing else in this armor works unless there is truth. Remember that Satan is a liar, and he is good at deceiving and deception. The girdle of truth holds everything together. It is the lifeline for the soldier. In today's army it is called the web gear, and it holds a soldier's canteen, ammo pouches, fanny pack and his first aid packet. With everything in it, it weighs about 80 pounds.

A Christian soldier's web gear holds the sword. This web gear or Girdle of Truth speaks of the Lord Jesus. He said. "...I am the way, the truth and the life. No man comes to the Father but by Me" (John 14:6). This verse has become important to me. Jesus is replying to Pilate in John18:37, when He says, "You say rightly that I am a king. For this cause I was born, and for this cause I have come into the world, that I should bear witness to the truth." Why did Jesus come into this world? We would say He came into the world to seek and save that which was lost, and He did that. But, we would say, He came into the world to give His life as a ransom for the many, and He did that as well. But I want to submit to you that perhaps the root and the basis for everything that we have to say about Jesus' reason for coming into the world is the one that He gave when he answered that question. "I [came] into the world that I should bear witness to the truth. Everyone who is of truth hears my voice." Who or what do you believe today? Do you believe the television, the internet or the books you read?

We live in a world that is full of the revision of history. Our textbooks today are completely out of line. Satan is a master at false philosophy and deception, and one of the things that is greatly needed today is to call this nation and this people back to the point of saying, "God's word is truth. It is absolute truth."

How do we know that lying and murder are wrong? They are wrong because they are against the character of God. God said to us, "Thou shalt not..." because it is against His character. It is not something somebody has dreamed up.

Some would like to take every reference to God out of our country. They would like to get rid of everything that has to do with the authority of the Word of God. A woman at a church in Montana where I once spoke said to me, "We were doing fine until you got here." She and a few others were in the business of deception, and they were trying to pirate the church. But the only place we can go to get absolute truth is to the revelation of God. I am not smart enough to come up with absolute truth, but God in His grace and mercy has given us everything that we need. The Bible is our final authority in all matters of faith and practice.

God thrusts us out into this world. It is a world that has gone awry, a world that is bent against God and His Christ, and a world that is full of deceit and dishonesty. He sends us forth as soldiers to carry the truth. We must be involved in telling the truth.

The second article is the "Breastplate of Righteousness." The breastplate that soldiers in Paul's day knew about was made of metal plates and chains that covered the body from the neck to the waist, both in the front and the back. I have heard some speakers and preachers say that the

Breastplate of Righteousness protects us as long as we are in the attack mode, but if we turn around and flee, we are vulnerable from the back. I want you to know we are covered front and back when we have to make a strategic withdrawal. It is important for us to understand that this breast plate of righteousness again speaks of Jesus Christ. He doesn't just cover a part of us, He covers all of us, and we never know where the attack is going to come from. Sometimes we can be riding down the road and be attacked. It might come from the airwaves. It might come from someone else. It might come from a thought that happens to penetrate into our heads, causing us to say, "Where did that thought come from?" The present-day soldier has absolutely no idea where the next attack will come from. It can come from a sniper's bullet, or it can come from any direction on the ground or in the air. We need complete body armor. God says, "I'm going to give you armor that will cover all of you. It will cover your front and your back. It symbolizes the righteousness of Christ."

Let me share some verses with you that convey this truth. "For He made Him who knew no sin to be sin for us, that we might become the righteousness of God in Him" (2 Corinthians 5:21). "Put on the new man which was created according to God, in true righteousness and holiness" (Ephesians 4:24). The life we live either fortifies us against Satan's attacks or makes us more vulnerable. Our activities, the people with whom we associate, the things that we want, and so many other things can expose us to Satan's attacks. "By the word of truth, by the power of God, by the armor of righteousness on the right hand and on the left" (2 Corinthians 6:7). Notice God's provision for us in these words. It is not mine; it is His. I am thankful for the righteousness of God that has been imputed to us. We did not earn it and we could not deserve it, but He gave it to us.

The sandals are the next item of the armor. Ephesians 6:14-15 says we are "to stand… having our feet shod with the preparation of the gospel of peace." The shoes soldiers wore in the Bible days were a type of hobnail sandal that gave better traction. That was needed for the soldier to withstand and then stand. Shoes are tremendously important.

I have a picture of an infantry sergeant who is sitting on the hillside in one of the worship services. He has his boots off and is rubbing his feet. He is saying, "Oh my poor feet." They were really bad because of all the humidity and heat. At the end of that service, he trusted Christ as his Savior. As the picture was taken he was looking at his feet, and his feet were giving out on him. This business of being ready has to do with preparation. Our daily task is to be ready to share the gospel. The sandals were for mobility. Perhaps you know what it is like when your feet give out on you. It affects the whole body. A good soldier of Christ needs to have the "Sandals of the Preparation of the Gospel." Peter put it this way in I Peter 3:15, "But sanctify the Lord God in your hearts, and always be ready to give a defense to everyone who asks you a reason for the hope that is in you, with meekness and fear."

In our next chapter, we are going to learn how to be ready for evangelism. I want to say to you that I am convinced that evangelism is caught not taught. If you want to help somebody be a soul winner, you just go out and show him how to do it. Often, when I start evangelism classes, the first week there are 50. The next week there are 40, and after one month, we are down to the faithful few because it is hard work. It takes discipline, and it takes commitment.

The shield was a two-foot by four-foot wood frame covered over with heavy leather. It had a fire retardant in it so it could quench all the fiery darts of the enemy. The soldiers also had a way to hook their shields together. They needed one another, and so do we. The devil is throwing fiery darts. Now, it smarts if they hit you, but we have this "Shield of Faith" for our protection. This is not just saving grace, but it is also living grace. We are not only saved by faith, but we walk by faith. "But without faith it is impossible to please Him, for he who comes to God must believe that He is, and that He is a rewarder of those who diligently seek Him" (Hebrews 11:6). We walk by faith and not by sight.

Next, we take the "Helmet of Salvation." The order in which the armor is given here is the same order that you would use to put your armor on in the Army. The last thing I ever put on in the Army was the helmet. When trouble comes you really appreciate that helmet. It protects you from fragments and from small caliber gun fire. Did you know the helmet is also used for cleansing? How many of you have taken a bath in your helmet? I have more than once. It becomes your bathtub. It is a place of cleansing. It protects the brain. It is really difficult to wear it except in times of danger. I am thankful that God has given us salvation. He has given us ability under God for the renewing of our minds. We know what Satan is up to. Paul puts it this way in Romans 12:1-2, "I beseech you therefore, brethren, by the mercies of God, that you present your bodies a living sacrifice, holy, acceptable to God, which is your reasonable service. And do not be conformed to this world, but be transformed by the renewing of your mind, that you may prove what is that good and acceptable and perfect will of God." We are all under construction, and God has given us a Helmet of Salvation. I assume that everyone reading this has made that choice to receive Christ as Savior, but this area of protecting the mind with the word of God is a continual project.

Is your armor in place? Let us talk about how we put it on. I think this is really the main focus. If we intend to put on the armor, how do we do it? We don't go to a supply room and get it. God has it already provided for us through his Son, the Lord Jesus. We put this armor on by a conscious effort to accept truth, righteousness, the gospel, faith and salvation. So let us put it on. How do we put it on? We put it on by prayer.

Heavenly Father,
Your solider prays for victory as he puts on Your provision of the armor. I claim by faith the whole armor of God.

I put on the girdle of truth!
I accept Your word as absolute truth. I refuse to submit to the lies of the Devil.

I put on the breastplate of righteousness!
Thank You for Your righteousness through the sacrifice of Your Son on the cross.

I put on the shoes of peace!
I prepare my heart to be ready to give a testimony of Your grace.

I take the shield of faith!
I accept Your protection by faith against the subtle attacks of Satan.

I put on the helmet of salvation!
I renew my mind by the Word of God so that I can be an effective solider.

I take the sword of the spirit!
I affirm by faith my trust in Your word so that I may submit to You and resist the evil one.

5

Our Offensive Weapons

I n our study today, we will discuss the G5, the Director of Civil Affairs, who tells us about our offensive weapons. Let's pray.

Father, how thankful we are that when You place us in a war zone, You give us first of all defensive armor, and secondly offensive weapons. We are thankful that these two offensive weapons are effective in changing the hearts of people. As You have said in Your Word, "We are not saved with corruptible things such as silver and gold for our vain conversation or lifestyle, but by the precious blood of Jesus Christ." So we are thankful to be able to claim that blood and to trust You to lead us during our study. In Jesus' name, amen.

We have two offensive weapons: the **Word of God** and **prayer**. Ephesians 6:17b-18 reads, "The sword of the Spirit, which is the word of God; praying always with all prayer and supplication in the Spirit, being watchful to this end with all perseverance and supplication for all saints."

The G5 gives his briefing in which he tells us how to win the hearts of the people. You can beat people down, but unless you win their hearts, you have failed. While serving with the 20th Engineer Battalion, I got rather close to a Vietnamese army chaplain who was a great man of God. Through him, I was able to get to know the national Christians in the city of Pleiku and then minister to them. They came to me one day and said,

"Our little church out here," which was not far from our post, "was bombed last night. The enemy came in and blew a side out of it. Could you help us?" So I went out and looked at it. I thought that it should be no problem and that we should be able to help. I went to my commander and asked if we could solve this situation. He said, "You get as many men as you can to volunteer, and you go out there and reconstruct that building." We had the materials so we went out and got to work. A week later, they had a much better building than they had prior to the attack, and it was a joy to be there when they had their dedication. The building was packed with believers.

Soon, the believers came and said, "We have another problem. The same enemy came the other night and blew the side out of our seminary building in Pleiku. Do you think you could help?" So I went back to my commander and told him the problem. "I need some more help and more material."

He agreed and said, "Perhaps this is the most important thing we have to do while we are here." That was interesting. My commander was a West Pointer who was a strong leader. He recognized that while we were there doing all those other duties, we had a responsibility to the national people.

You may have heard of Dr. Victor Barnett. He served many years in China as a missionary. He was a little man whose hands were curled because of arthritis. One day he was addressing us preacher-boys, and he stuck out his crooked finger at us and said, "Gentlemen, I want you to know that we don't have to defend the word of God. We just have to use it." I am thankful for apologists who are great men of learning and study for the defense of the Gospel. I am thankful for men like Ravi Zacharias and others who have taken the position of defending the historic faith. I am also very thankful that God has called us to take His sword and use it. We need to use it in the winning of the hearts of people.

Paul said to Timothy in 1 Timothy 1:18-19, "This charge I commit to you, son Timothy, according to the prophecies previously made concerning you, that by them you may wage the good warfare, having faith and a good conscience, which some having rejected, concerning the faith have suffered shipwreck." Paul once again reiterated the power of our offensive weapons in 2 Timothy 2:15. "Study to show yourself approved unto God; a workman that needs not to be ashamed, rightly dividing the word of Truth." It takes study. Often we are bashful about witnessing because we are afraid somebody will ask us something we cannot answer. We need to be people of the Word.

Second Timothy 3:16-17 reads, "All Scripture is given by inspiration of God, and is profitable for doctrine, for reproof, for correction, for instruction in righteousness, that the man of God may be complete, thoroughly equipped for every good work." The Scripture tells us what to believe, and we desperately need that in the day and age in which we live. People need to be taught the truth of the Word of God. It tells us where we are wrong and how to change and how to live. I think small groups can be very beneficial, but sometimes those who attend them get together and just pool their ignorance. We need to come back to solid teaching on doctrine which is what we are to believe.

We need reproof which points out where we have sinned. Can you remember a time when the Word of God brought reproof in your life? We called that conviction. We knew we were sinners and that we had disobeyed a holy, righteous God. We knew we stood in judgment.

Lastly, the Word of God will instruct us on how we should live. That is what instruction in righteousness is. No matter how long we have been believers, we keep learning from God's truth.

I want to share the power of the Word through a couple of illustrations. The first is when I was in the pit of despair. Two months into the my 12-month Vietnam tour, I was so miserable I would have been glad to have been shot, as long as it did not kill me, so I could go home. I had left a wife and four kids at home. I had a commander who would not show up for any religious events other than memorial services. I had an executive officer who would always say to me when I came to staff meetings, "Well, how many souls did you save today, Chaplain?"

It was interesting to me that when I ran into him a few years later, I was the same rank as he was. I said to him, "Do you remember what you used to say to me?" He had forgotten about it, but I reminded him.

So out of a thousand men, I would have maybe a dozen to 15 men in the services throughout the week. My expectations were not being met. You all have heard the phrase, "There is no atheist in the foxhole." That was not proving true. I was serving men who were dismissing the reality of death.

I thought that perhaps I could get a daily Bible study going, so we made a big poster and put it up by the chow or mess tent. I started the daily Bible study. I had one man, a sergeant, come, and he really did not come to learn. He came to debate me. We did discuss the Scripture, and pretty soon he started bringing a PFC with him who also wanted to debate. So now it was two against one. They were having fun. I knew they looked forward to it, and I looked forward to the opportunity to challenge them with the Word of God.

We went out on a major mission, and when the battalion went out, the chaplain went out with them. My position was with the aid station. During the combat, my first student, the sergeant, was killed. My whole world came crashing down. I was grumbling and complaining, and I was bitter against God. I said, "God, I felt I was following You when I joined the chaplaincy, and I felt like I followed You all the way. I have done everything I can do."

The PFC was wounded, and about 10 days later, he came back to me and said, "Chaplain, I've got to tell you what happened." He had another story for me. He said, "You know the sergeant and I gave you a hard time."

I said, "Yeah you did." He said, "I want you to know what happened the night before we went out on that mission. We knew that we were going into a hostile place, and both of us got out those tracts or those Bible study things that you gave us. We got on our knees and we asked Christ to be our Savior. Every word that you had spoken to us was like a fire on our souls and hit against us like a hammer." They did not know Jeremiah 23:29 which reads "Is not My word like a fire? says the Lord and like a hammer that breaks the rock in pieces?" I would never have known that had he not come back. God straightened me out that day because then I really understood my responsibility. After that time, more came to every service, and men were saved. The last six months was the most exciting time I have ever had in the ministry. Instead of preaching to 12-15 men, I was preaching to 600 men per week. We had marvelous things going on, but I want you to see the power of that sword.

I have one more illustration. I was serving in the National Guard. We had a new commander who had just taken over our unit. He had a PhD degree and had a very responsible position in civilian life. He came to a service because he was a new commander. That Sunday, I preached on Colossians. I remember that because I remember preaching in Colossians about the family. When the service was over, he came up to me and said, "Would you show me how to find that passage in the Bible?"

I knew this man had a PhD, but he did not know how to use an index to find Colossians. I found it for him, gave it to him, and said, "Why don't you keep the New Testament."

He responded, "I don't want it. I'm a humanist, and I don't feel I need it. But," he said, "I found your talk interesting."

When someone calls what I said "a talk," I know I have a candidate for salvation. The next month, we were together again. I always put Gideon New Testaments out on the seats, and the colonel came and picked one up. I remember I was preaching from 2 Peter 3. I gave the page number so he could find it.

Afterward, he came up to me and said, "May I keep this New Testament?"

I said, "Yes sir!"

The next month we were in the field at Grayling, Michigan. He sat really close by with a general beside him. My chaplain's assistant was sitting on the other side of me where he could see the commander. My assistant, who later became a chaplain, said to me after the service, "The Lord is opening the colonel's eyes."

I never expected that God would do something in his life. I just did not expect it. The next time we were together was for the two-week army training in Grayling. He came into my room and closed the door and began to cry. He said, "I don't want to do this in front of my men. Would you make an appointment with me to meet me at the chapel?"

I replied, "Yes sir."

Whatever your commander wants done, you do it! We met at the chapel, and he said to me, "Before I came to annual training I went to the best counselor at the university, and I told him my problem." The counselor could not help. The commander said to me, "I know you can." He went on to explain to me that he had had an affair with a secretary in his office. He was going to lose his job and his family. His military career was all washed up. Contrary to common belief, the Army does believe in morality. This was a problem for a man who was a rising star destined to be a general.

After he told me the whole story, I went through the plan of salvation with him and asked him if he felt the need to cry out to God for mercy.

He said, "Yes, I do." I said, "Why don't we kneel here." I thought it was a good time and place for a colonel to do that.

He got down on his knees, and he cried out to God and asked for forgiveness. He got up from his knees and took that little New Testament and turned to the back of it. There is a place in the back to sign and date when you have been saved. He immediately turned there without any coaching, signed his name, and dated it.

He asked, "Would you and your wife be willing to meet with my wife?"

I responded that we would certainly be glad to do that.

He said, "Before you do that, I need to make a call. May I use your phone?"

He called his wife and said, "I want you to know how sorry I am for my sin and I ask your forgiveness. I've asked God for forgiveness, and I've given my heart to Christ. I'd like for you to come this weekend and meet my chaplain and his wife."

He had planned on meeting up with his girlfriend on the weekend. He went on to ask if he could make one more call. He called her and he said, "What we have done is so wrong. I've sinned against you. I've sinned against my body. I've sinned against my family, and I've sinned against God. The relationship with you is done. Do not come this weekend."

Ruth and I could not wait until his wife got there; we thought we would have another one to whom we could tell the good news of the gospel and were excited to see what would happen.

Well she came and we shared with her. But she said, "At 18 years old I went home from college with a Baptist girl. I went to church with her, and at the invitation I went forward and I asked Christ to be my Savior. For the 18 years that we have been married, I have pleaded with him to go to a Bible teaching church, but he would never go." She forgave him and their marriage was restored.

I want you to see the power of the sword. The most unlikely candidate for grace that I have ever known, in the matter of four months, went from denying the Word and declaring himself to be a humanist to faith in Christ. Every military staff person carries a notebook. On top of his notebook was the New Testament.

Our last offensive weapon is prayer. We are told in scripture, "Praying always with all prayer and supplication in the spirit; watching thereunto with all perseverance and supplication for all saints." I daresay all Christians believe in prayer, and many have seen the power of prayer over and over again. Yet it seems as though we somehow need to refocus on it as an offensive weapon. We are to pray without ceasing. We are to pray with all kinds of prayer, and 1 Timothy 2:1 says, "Therefore I exhort first of all that supplications, prayers, intercessions, and giving of thanks be made for all men." It is interesting that he categorized those for us.

The word supplication is an earnest request, knowing our helplessness. We just cry out with supplication, "Lord we cannot do anything about this; It is out of our control." Or, "We are pleading for your mercy and for your grace." The word prayer means a humble request. "I have no right to ask, but I come believing that you have asked me to come. I come pleading for your grace." The word, intercession, is a conversation. It is standing face-to-face and in place of another.

Have you ever been in a place where you could hardly pray? I have. You ask for someone else to pray with you and maybe pray for you. We do that often when we pray for those outside the body of Christ. They have no standing to pray, but we do. We ask that God might direct in their lives. We intercede for them, asking the Lord to bring them to faith in Christ or that He would meet their other needs. I have seen Christians so overwhelmed with pain or so overwhelmed with deep depression that they just could not pray.

Paul wrote that we are to give thanks and praise. We are greatly blessed when we praise and thank the Lord. Ephesians 6:18 reads, "Praying always with all prayer and supplication in the Spirit, being watchful to this end with all perseverance and supplication for all the saints." Philippians 4:6 says, "Be anxious for nothing, but in everything by prayer and supplication, with *thanksgiving*, let your requests be made known to God; and the peace of God, which surpasses all understanding, will guard your hearts and minds through Christ Jesus."

We are told to pray in the Spirit. When we struggle to express ourselves and we cannot find the words for our thoughts, is it not wonderful how the Holy Spirit Himself helps us when we pray?

We are to pray with our eyes open. The Scripture often admonishes us to watch and pray. We need to know what is going on around us. We have to watch. We need to know what is happening in our government, we need to know what is happening at our church, we need to know what is happening in our families, and we need to understand our relationships with one another. We pray in that sense with our eyes open. Mark records Jesus saying, "Watch therefore, for you do not know when the master of the house is coming—in the evening, at midnight, at the crowing of the rooster, or in the morning—lest, coming suddenly, he find you sleeping. And what I say to you, I say to all: Watch!"

I want to give you some quotes concerning prayer that have been a challenge to me:

"Men may spurn our appeals, reject our message, oppose our arguments, despise our persons - but they are helpless against our prayers." (J. Sidlow Baxter)

"I'd rather teach one man to pray than ten men to preach." (J.H.Jowett)

"I never prayed sincerely for anything but it came, at some time...somehow, in some shape." (Adoniram Judson)

"I have so much to do today, that I shall spend the first three hours in prayer." (Martin Luther)

There are men of prayer who have been inspiring examples to me:

George Müeller has proven to the world the truth of Philippians 4:19, "But my God shall supply all your needs according to his riches in glory by Christ Jesus." He will always be remembered as the man who got things from God. His testimony is an inspiration to Christians everywhere. When he died, in March 1898, he had obtained from God more than anyone else who had ever lived: seven and a half million dollars in today's money to use in God's work.

Will Houghton, in preaching the funeral of R.A. Torrey said, "Those who knew him intimately knew him as man of regular and uninterrupted prayer. He knew what it meant to pray without ceasing. With hours set systematically apart for prayer, he gave himself diligently to this ministry."

We find it difficult to pray because it is work. It is warfare. There are times when in our prayer time we are battling the forces of evil. We must come to the place of submission to God and to a total trust in Him.

In conclusion, we only have two offensive weapons, but they are enough. We do not need anything else. Second Corinthians 10:3-4 says, "For though we walk in the flesh, we do not war according to the flesh. For the weapons of our warfare are not carnal but mighty in God for pulling down strongholds, casting down arguments and every high thing that exalts itself against the knowledge of God, bringing every thought into captivity to the obedience of Christ."

The two weapons, God's Word and prayer, will do everything that God wants to accomplish in your life and my life.

In closing let us again pray.

Heavenly Father,
Your solider prays for victory as he puts on Your provision of the armor. I claim by faith the whole armor of God.
I put on the girdle of truth!
I accept Your word as absolute truth. I refuse to submit to the lies of the Devil.
I put on the breastplate of righteousness!

Thank You for Your righteousness through the sacrifice of Your Son on the cross.

I put on the shoes of peace!

I prepare my heart to be ready to give a testimony of Your grace.

I take the shield of faith!

I accept Your protection by faith against the subtle attacks of Satan.

I put on the helmet of salvation!

I renew my mind by the Word of God so that I can be an effective solider.

I take the sword of the spirit!

I affirm by faith my trust in Your word so that I may submit to You and resist the evil one.

Now, onward to the battle!

Acknowledgements

Thank you to those who encouraged me to write this book. I especially thank those who spent time making this book a reality: my wife, Ruth, for helping to get this into print; our son, Paul, for technical help, our grandson, Zach Ripley, for proofing the material; my pastor, Robert Smith, for reading and making corrections, our son, Brigadier General Phil Owens, for helping with the military proofing, and Andy Van Loenen for editing and page formatting.

About the Author

Chaplain Cliff Owens became a believer as a 20-year-old. On his 21st birthday he began preaching in his home church as a student pastor. He was graduated from Grand Rapids Baptist College and Seminary in 1963.

While pastoring Lincoln Ave. Baptist in Ionia, Michigan the Lord called him to serve in the U.S. Army. Having received his endorsement from the General Association of Regular Baptist Churches in 1967 he began his 26-years of ministry as an army chaplain. In 1968-69 he served as a battalion chaplain in Viet Nam. And after completing a 3-year commitment he once again went back into the pastorate. He immediately joined the Michigan Army National Guard where he served as battalion, brigade and state chaplain. During his final 2-years of service he served as a liaison to the Florida Army National Guard.

Chaplain Owens and his wife of 59-years have four children who all were a vital part of the pastoral and chaplain ministries. It was a total team ministry.

While teaching a Sunday school class on Ephesians, many class members asked him to put this material into print. It has been used of the Lord to encourage and instruct His saints. His prayer is that this material will help you to be a good soldier of Jesus Christ.

Made in the USA
Monee, IL
07 April 2023